Let's Find Out About

Toothpaste

by Kathy Barabas

LET'S FIND OUT
BOOKS

Scholastic Inc.
Toronto   London   Auckland   Sydney

We are grateful to Tom's of Maine for the opportunity to
photograph this book at their factory in Kennebunk, Maine.
Special thanks to Regis Park for her generous help.

Photographs by John Williams
Cover photograph by David Vesey
Illustrations by Ellen Joy Sasaki
Design by Alleycat Design, Inc.

Photographs: p. 3: Ana Esperanza Nance; p. 4: Oranges, Benelux Press/Photo Researchers;
Cliffs, Lynn McLaren/Photo Researchers; Seaweed, Dale E. Boyer/Photo Researchers. p. 20: David Vesey;
p. 21: (from top left to bottom right) Janes Levin, John Fortunato, James Levin (3), David Vesey.

Library of Congress Cataloging-in-Publication Data
Barabas, Kathy, 1945-
    Let's find out about toothpaste / by Kathy Barabas; photographs by John Williams;
  [illustrations by Ellen Joy Sasaki].
        p. cm. — (Let's find out library)
      Summary: Illustrations and simple text describe the process of making toothpaste, from combining
  the raw ingredients to shipping the packaged tubes to the store.
  ISBN 0-590-36777-3
  1. Toothpaste — Juvenile literature.   [1. Toothpaste.
  2. Manufactures.]   I. Williams, John, 1963- ill.   II. Sasaki, Ellen Joy, ill.   III. Title. IV. Series
  TP955.B37 1997
  668'.55—dc21   96-47546
                                                                                    CIP
                                                                                     AC

Brush! Brush! Brush!

What's in this stuff?
How does it get into that
squishy tube?

Let's find out!

3

calcium carbonate

seaweed

Toothpaste is made from water,
plants, and other things found in nature.

4

Some of them
make it taste good.

mint

5

Factory workers shake and pour everything into a giant mixer.

Water shoots in through a pipe.
The big lid snaps down and . . .

Swoosh!
The beaters go to work.
It's like making a huge cake.

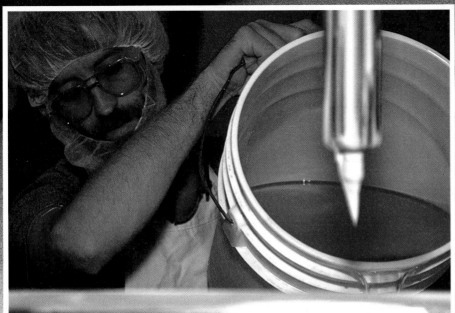

Next, workers **mix** in the flavoring.

This batch will be orange-flavored.

Then they scrape. They won't waste a drop!
The toothpaste is ready.

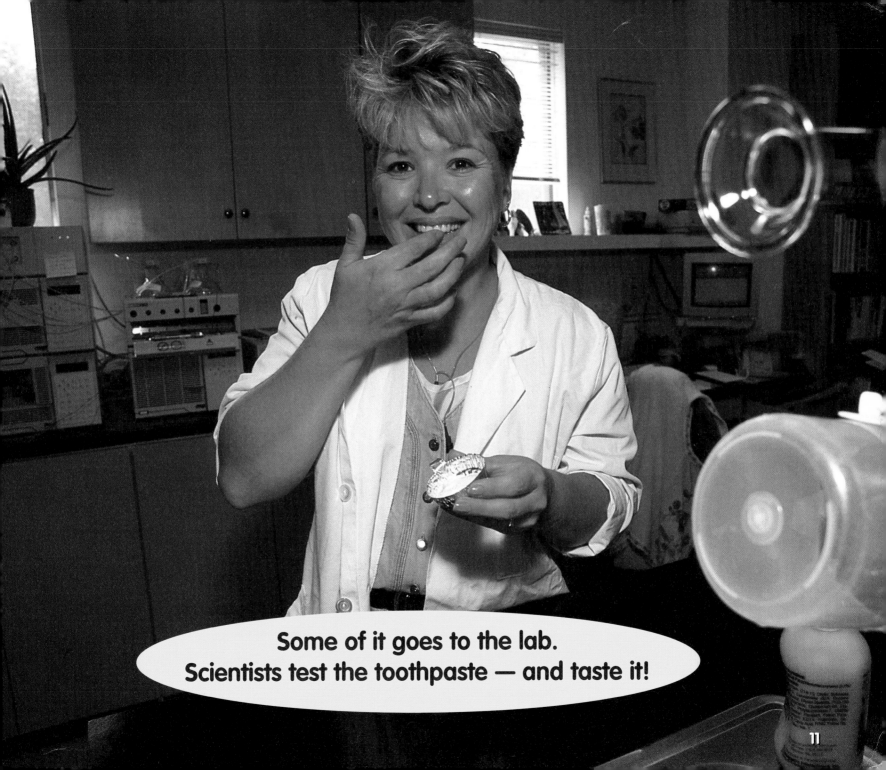

Some of it goes to the lab.
Scientists test the toothpaste — and taste it!

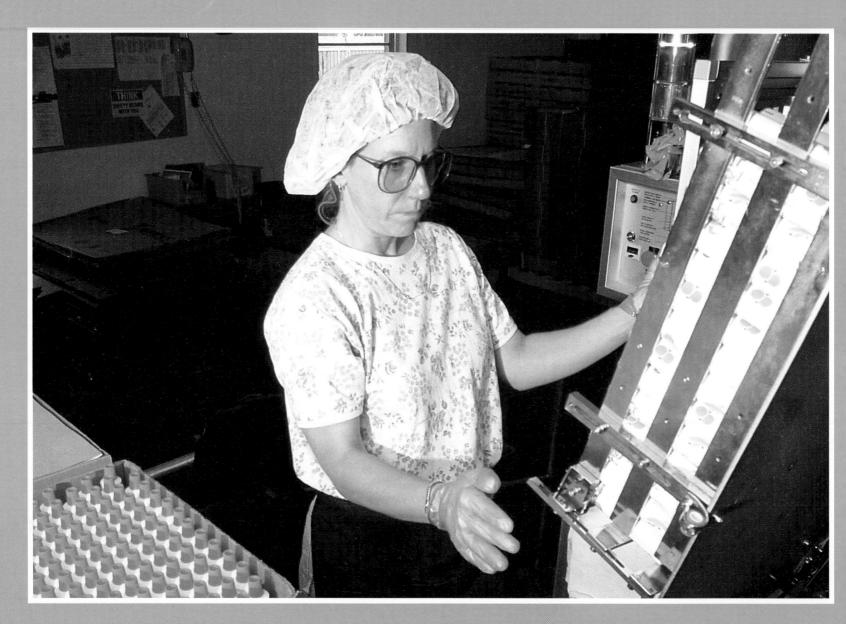

Now the toothpaste goes to this filling machine.
A worker puts in the empty tubes.

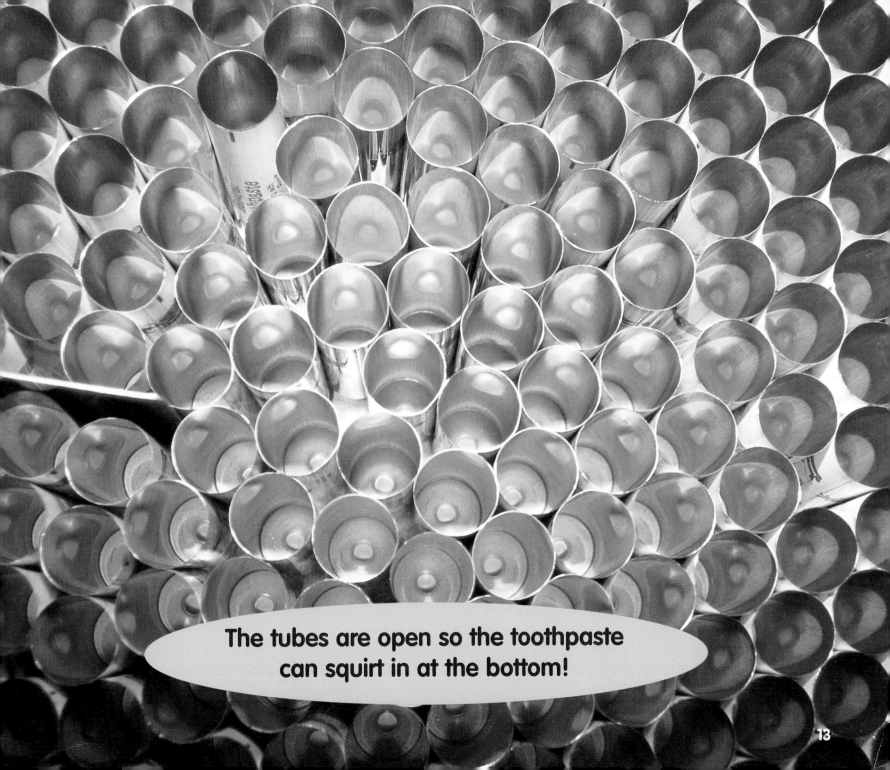

The tubes are open so the toothpaste can squirt in at the bottom!

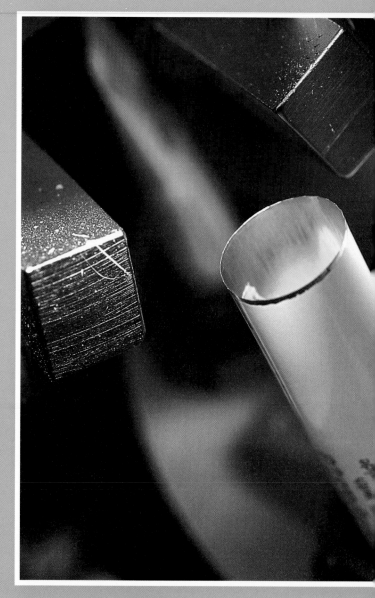

The toothpaste
shoots into the tube.

SQUEEZE!

A machine folds the bottom and seals it tight.

The full tubes slide out — about 80 whiz
by every minute! They are ready to be boxed.

Workers fill the toothpaste boxes, two at a time.

The boxes are packed into big cartons for shipping...

... and the toothpaste
is on its way to the store,
then to your home ...

Smile!

Let's Find Out About
Toothpaste!

Start Here

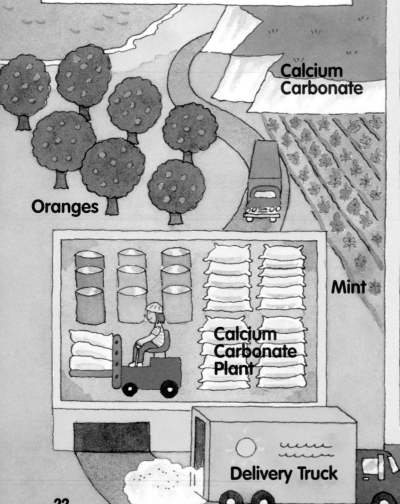

Oranges

Calcium Carbonate

Mint

Calcium Carbonate Plant

Delivery Truck

Tubes

Filling Machine

Mixer

Water

Filling Mixer

Laboratory

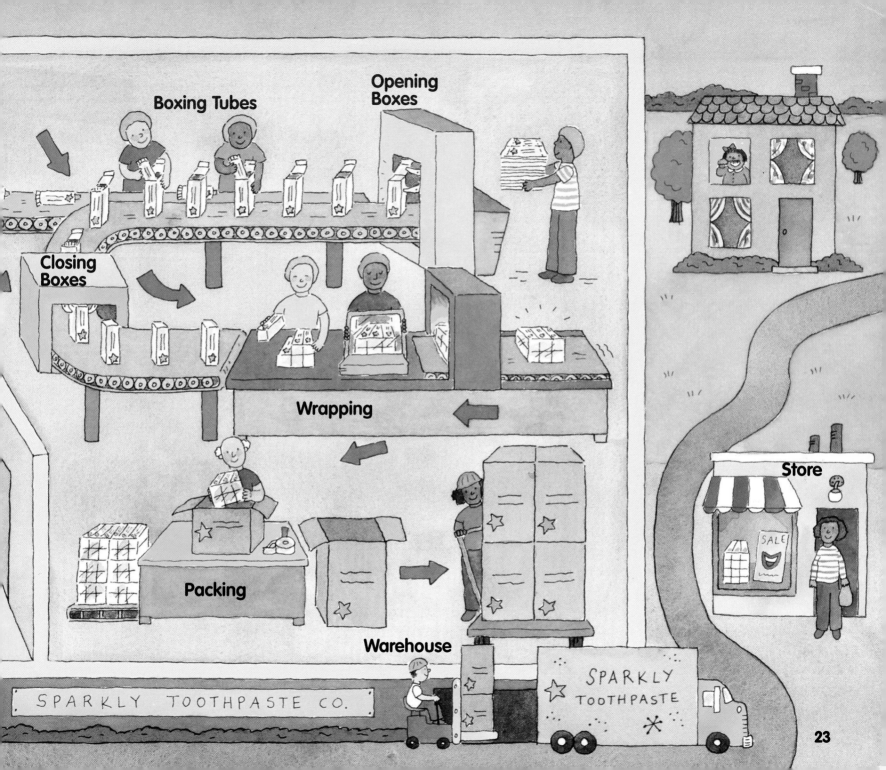

Boxing Tubes

Opening Boxes

Closing Boxes

Wrapping

Packing

Warehouse

Store

SPARKLY TOOTHPASTE CO.

SPARKLY TOOTHPASTE

SALE

23

Things to Do

Before reading, find a tube of toothpaste. Look at it and discuss it together: "What do you think toothpaste is made of? How can we find out? How do they get the toothpaste into the tube?" Children may enjoy reviewing (and revising!) their guesses after reading.

Read and reread!

Read once through the whole story. Then reread, taking time to look closely at each picture and talk about it.

Retell the sequence of making and packaging toothpaste. Use the illustration on pages 22–23 to help you tell the story.

Make up toothpaste commercials! Act out your own commercials. What's the name of your toothpaste? What makes it great? What will make people want to buy it?

Role-play a trip to the dentist. Take turns playing dentist and patient. Have fun setting up a pretend dental chair and instruments and giving very professional care!